AN ITALIAN VISIT

AN ITALIAN VISIT

by

C. DAY LEWIS

'. . . an Italian visit is a voyage of discovery,
not only of scenes and cities, but also of the
latent faculties of the traveller's heart and
mind. . .'

JASPER MORE: *The Land of Italy*

HARPER & BROTHERS PUBLISHERS
NEW YORK

AN ITALIAN VISIT

Printed in the United States of America

Contents

*All of this poem except Part V was written
during 1948-9*

To
HENRY REED

AN ITALIAN VISIT

I. Dialogue at the Airport

TOM   So here we are, we three, bound on a new
                                                experience.

DICK   Three persons in one man, bound for the Eternal
                                                City.

HARRY   We're not as young as we were, but Italy's
                                        some years older.

TOM   Listen, I don't much fancy antiques myself;
                                        we've had some.
Ruins fetch nothing today. The Forum, the Farringdon
                                                Market,
The Colosseum, Hiroshima – death's death, however you
                                        look at it,
However composed the remains. Time enough for such
                                        bric-à-brac when
My silver cord is loosed, my arches are fallen. Oh no, if
It's ruins you're after, we'll soon be parting company.

DICK   Wait!
There are ruins and ruins. Some mature their memories,
                                        feed them
On seeding love-spores blown from age to age; or it may be
Their ghosts fly back like a silver skein of doves when the
                                                crash
Of the fall that tumbled them out has died away. It is
                                        these ghosts
I'm going to look for.

13

HARRY   You think so. But I don't think you will find them.

The only ghosts I believe in are the dangerous self-detachments
We leave behind in places captured or captivating:
Garrisons, call them, or hostages – wiped out soon enough, most of them,
Yet here and there a hardier self lives on to haunt us
With the old riddle, what is the phantom, what the real.
Temple, aqueduct, belvedere, projects fulfilled or abandoned –
Multiform are the ruins, but the ghosts are always the same ghost.

TOM   We'd better leave you behind, then, to the desk, the queue and the rush-hour,
Men and women straphanging like clusters of bats, the bodies
That jostle and never touch, the eyes without speculation
But for tomorrow's headline or deadline; leave you behind
With all the white-faced addicts of a patent, cellophaned future.
London's the place for ghosts, if ghosts are invalid monads.
And for God's sake, Harry, don't tell us a crowd is always the same crowd.

DICK   What are we leaving behind, though? The identity cards that inform us
Not who we are or might be, but how we are interchangeable;
The season tickets that rattle us back and forth in a groove from

14

Centre to circumference, from dust to dust; the ration
books
Entitling each to his cut of the communal mess and heart-
burn.
The fog, the slush, the slogans.

HARRY   Italy will provide
The same slogans, no doubt, but at least in another language.

    TOM   No doubt in another language escapism may sound
more attractive.

    DICK   Well, it's a holiday, isn't it? Even Harry can take
a holiday.

    HARRY   I have omitted to pack my Kierkegaard, Marx
and Groddeck.
My *angst* I can only hope they will confiscate at the Customs.

    TOM   I am too old to suppose new facts give new sensa-
tions:
Still, like shadows, our senses revive on a shot of sunshine.
One would go far to feel their primitive dance again

    DICK   Far from the heart's last ditch, the stand on private
relationships

    HARRY   Far from the mind's closed shop and the intellec-
tual weeklies.

    TOM   So here we are, we three, off for a fortnight's
holiday,
Our fingers already reaching out to the treat before us

    DICK   Like a child's on Christmas Eve who, visioning the
dear morrow
Spangled with expectation, would whip time faster and
faster,

And at last whips himself into a humming sleep.

HARRY   Travel ought to be sleep – I mean, we should
move oblivious
To the interspace between here and there. We've only a
limited
Stock of attention, and this we had better not spend on
wayside
Sirens who'd make us break our journey or regret not
breaking it.

TOM   If he means what I think he means, I am not to
look out of the window.

DICK   There's something in what he says, though the
motive's unsound, as usual.
Could the zone between here and there be instead a kind
of hiatus,
Heart would be spared the throes of departure and anticipa-
tion,
The tug-of-war in the tensile flesh between near and far,
The sense of all routes leading to a scheduled anti-climax
Because what they lead away from seems now, too late, the
nonpareil
The truly virgin place.

HARRY   Yes, travel is travail: a witless
Ordeal of self-abasement to an irreversible process.
It would be nice, waking as it were from twilight sleep, to
Find the new bourne beside one.

TOM   But you never can skip the process
And reach a conclusion, the one is woven into the other
Like hues of a shot-silk rainbow: apart from which, your
analogy

Falls to the ground – we shall not, I presume, give birth to
Italy.

DICK   But we should give body to our so tentative view-
points of it

HARRY   Or rather conceive a self, hitherto inconceivable,
through it.

TOM   Both of you ask too much. I'll be quite happy,
taking

Snapshots.

DICK   I shall develop and print them.

HARRY   I shall mount them.
And after a year or two fetching the album out again,
Snapshot or time exposure, in every scene, among each
group
Posed before pillars, informally strolling across a piazza,
We'll see, oh yes we shall see them, the usual boring
intruders –
Spirits or ectoplasm, who cares? – spoiling the brilliant
Occasion like long-lost cousins or hangovers out of the
future.
Whether from Dick's chemicals or Tom's automatic choice
Of the haunted subject.

TOM   I don't deny my photographs would be
More satisfactory if you two could stop interfering.
What with Dick's fancy touches and Harry's insufferable
habit
Of scribbling captions across them which later become
obsessions –
Spirits or ectoplasm, who cares? – no wonder if
The results are not

DICK   There would be no results but for my dark-room,
Where negatives lie steeped in a warm solution, passing
The acid test of Lethe, to emerge with the self-assurance
Of memories; but for this hand that ever so lightly brushes
Over your brash impressions the dove-downed, hallowing
haze.
What if I do touch up now and then a defective feature? –
There is no law against putting the best face on experience.

HARRY   No law to say we must grind the cornfields into
vitamins,
Reduce the grape to a formula, express the olive in terms of
Statistics. It is deplorable, yes, and against nature:
Nevertheless, one does it, being of a generation
Whose only faith is the piling of fact on fact, in the hope
that
Some day a road may be built of them and may lead some-
where.

TOM   In the meanwhile, we go to Italy: Dick, with his
decadent craving
For perfection at any price, who cannot pass by an arc
Without officiously filling in the rest of the circle;
Harry whose conscience bids him take the round world to
pieces
And ticket each stone for the use of a possibly grateful
posterity;
And I who, with your permission, intend just to enjoy
myself.

DICK   But even you have been taught the simpler
associations –
For example, mouth and famine, lily and corpse, bambino

And bomb – to say nothing of *odi et amo* – which stand in
the light of
Enjoyment pure and simple. Travellers can't be choosers
Any more than the stay-at-homes.

HARRY   No, man's gleaming aspirations
Are endlessly batted down as telegraph wire by the poles
When you look from a train window, everywhere and for
ever
Abased his soaring creeds by the very proofs which support
them.
Yet still we aspire. Each journey's a bid for the empyrean
Of Absolute freedom, whether we fly to the ends of the earth
Or take a week-end ticket to Clacton; and as certainly
We are twitched back on the thread reeled out from our
ruling passion.

TOM   All the more reason for going abroad with a *tabula
rasa,*
Not trailing clouds of vainglory or the old tin can of con-
science.
Granted we cannot entirely escape ourselves, and granted
That up to a point we can only see what we're bound to
look for,
Still, there is such a thing as simple impressionability,
A sense in which form and colour are more than mere
dreams of our senses,
A moment – though rare – when the lily speaks for itself
alone
And the babe's ephemeral laughter chimes with eternity.

DICK   And another thing: when the new place, mysteri-
ously conveying

A promise of maiden surrender and morning glory, invites
us,
We are wax in her hands for a little, our former loves
effaced,
Ready to take her seal, to believe the rewarding fallacy
That this is it at last, that this time all will be different;
And we really may find the knack of pure freedom, pure
submission,
Whereby a miraculous rebirth is possible – find it
Before the displaced selves crowd back to declare us
impotent.

HARRY Since you two appear in agreement on this, the
logical next step
Is to unpack our preconceptions and leave them behind here,
Discarding whatever might come between us and the naked
fact.

TOM Myself, I have always travelled light – eyes, ears,
nose, fingers,
And one thing more, I carry. Now Dick, you'll have to
jettison
Time, whose ripple prettifies the weed which fouls it, and
flaws
The willow it images.

DICK Time, without which there could be no images? –
You might as well go abroad without an interpreter – you,
Tom,
Who don't know a word in any tongue but your own. Now
Harry
Has much he should lighten his bag of; props, probes and
provisos;

The impressive manner he wears while wooing the heiress,
Truth;
And of course the instruments he will presently use to
dissect her.

HARRY   Your programmes are too ambitious. I only
meant to suggest
We should expose the Italy faked by our fraudulent vision,
Tear up the glowing prospectus that pictured a heaven on
earth

TOM   Confess why we are going and what we expect to
find there?

DICK   Rub out the shadow our ego projects? Make a clean
sheet of Italy?

HARRY   Yes, a cadenza from each on this fantasy movement. We have
Ten minutes until our flight-number is called. Let Tom
begin.

TOM   First, a great Elgarian clash and bray of sunshine
Throwing open the day, blaring a paeony fanfare
Through flesh and blood, throwing wide the earth – a
fabulous mansion
Where every maid is a gift, every moment a pulse in a
fun-fair.
None of your fairy gold! The real, royal, vulgar pageant –
Time flung like confetti or twirled in rosettes – was never
too garish
For me. How much better than your dim flounderings
toward some imagined
Immortal star, to flare like a firework and goldenly perish!
Mornings, I ask a cloudless sky; or if clouds there must be,

Billowy suds that have scoured the sky bluer than corn-
flowers:
Acacia and lemon-blossom shall drench me, mimosa dust
me,
Violet and rose be banked along my sauntering hours.
Noon shall stand as long as I fancy, and tall as houses –
A fountain pluming itself upon the enchanted air:
Afternoon shall sleep with the goat-flock villages drowsing
Lightly, precipice-high, or deep in shuttered squares.
Ah, but the nights! I see them festooned in a long fiesta –
Mediterranean nights that will send me spinning and flying
With the waltz of a purple Maelstrom, the arrowy glide of a
Cresta.
Here's to the masks and the music, the dancers ebbing and
flowing!
Let fairy-lit streets run wine through the veins like a ride
on a scenic
Railway! and then the ravishing flesh of girls consume me
Flame upon flame to scented ashes, and I a phoenix!
Yes, one thing I know: it's the sting of strangeness renews
me.
Listen, the bells tumble from a humming campanile
With a dull pot-and-pan clang: those two at the table – the
cadence
Is unfamiliar they talk in: banal their gist, but to me they
Are speaking, lover and carillon, with the tongues of angels.
I do not wish to dig down to the sullen roots of existence
Where one clod's the same as the next, or to tangle myself
in humanity's
Fretted heart-strings: not here lies the world of essential
difference,

But above, in the bloom, the spectrum, the transient
flavours and vanities.
Therefore I'd browse on the skin of things, the delicate
field of
Diversity, skimming gold from the buttercup, dust from
the nettle.
I, the merely sensual man, have a scope undreamed of
By you whom a larger ambition drives to discard or belittle
Appearance. And so I ask of Italy nothing more than
Mere foreignness, the shock and buoyant feel of the
unknown,
And quivering over its surface an iridescent path, an
Arrow to point me, the eternal tripper, away from home.

DICK   Different my nature, my needs. I journey as a
colonial
Reaching across generations to find the parent stock,
As a child setting out to colour a black-and-white picture
book,
A priest entering into the spirit of dead ceremonial . . .
They have been dormant so long, the ghosts that were used
to school us:
Deep-buried as once Pompeii the classroom walls with their
jaded
Photos of classical ruin, of statues leprous, abraded.
Did ever those dry bones live? And instantly Ovid, Catullus
Wild for his Lesbia, Virgil, Lucretius – sports of a prosy
Marble-eyed, muscle-bound people – emerge from the
shades to claim one.
Ancestor worship's a form of self-seeking: all the same, one
Is grateful to those who had no immediate hand in our crazy

Present: the Romans at any rate did manage to keep the
peace,
Off and on. But that's by the way. Some breathing counter-
part
I want for a dead language years ago learnt by heart,
Some vista shaped and haunted by youthful pieties.
Immortal landscape of a day, for ever dreaming
In haze of summers half imagined, half remembered!
Meek-swarded, comely pastoral where nymph and shepherd
Still twine two worlds in a dance! Demesne of phantoms,
teeming
With myrtle, vine and olive, pied with fact and fable!
Hero, god, or brute, all hold to the light their antique
Self-sufficiency – a grace which no romantic
Yearnings can discompose nor withering years enfeeble.
Such is the foreground. Behind it vaporously writhes a
spectacular
Region of mounting disquiet, dark meaning, where lie
concealed
A lake that shoots down birds with a whiff of the under-
world;
Proserpine's trapdoor; a gorge rumbling in tones oracular;
A forest of shadows juddering athwart the golden bough.
Is it I they wait for, the feudal lords of light and mystery
Their kingdoms to unite? Is it they who shall assist me
To define, or abolish, the frontier between my Then and my
Now?
There was a time of substance and shadow richly confused,
When a dry Tuscan evelight engraved the cricket-ground
And my study shafted towards the black diamonds and
dene profound

Of Pluto: then the beam went, the pit fell into disuse.
If I could find that place where nymph and shepherd meet
And the distance melts into deity, I would unearth my
buried
Heirlooms, my sealed orders. Genius of the place, remarry
These sundered elements, make one circle at last complete!

HARRY   A landscape I also may look for: a town in fiesta
would do
Equally well for the purpose this traveller has in view.
Let me try to explain myself – both artist and analyst;
hence
For me the approach that in others would be pure innocence
Were wild irresponsibility. Think! The desirable villa
Haunted by princes, hallowed with cypresses, there on a
hillside
Ultimately reduces to a vulgar hop of electrons:
I see the revellers, masked and articulated for faction;
Your language of bells and lovers I hear, but as workable
fictions.
Since all strips down to motion, and all's in a state of
becoming,
Whoever would master the truth by which your provoca-
tive, charming
Strip-tease universe lives, ideally should be at rest
Himself; at any rate disinterested, unimpressed.
And that is why I am far from being a keen traveller.
On the other hand, I admit one cannot hope to unravel
Experience unless one is to a certain degree involved.
Is there a method by which, then, a mutable self may
resolve

And fix the ever-changing? Let us try an experiment –
briefly
The playing a trick on time. Help me, you two, to achieve
it.
To see as it were from the far end of a cypress walk of
bereavement,
Or the eyrie of ten years hence! For look, how the terraced
garden,
Statues, orange trees, villa, unfocused now by sudden
Tremors – the whole prospect fidgets, vibrates, wavers,
Collapsing always with the present. But if upon that
fevered
Hill brow, my brow, should once be laid grief's cooling
hand,
Dance and dissolution would come to a dead stand.
Memory needs time before the outraged dwelling, love's
centre,
Purified, tear upon tear, shines forth like a shell of candour,
And all around, elegiac in evergreen, new contours
Idealize the old agony. But I have to induce
Years from a moment: therefore I must predicate loss.
Let me take some figure of the dance, so fleetingly, fiercely
exulting
That it quickens the seed of loss, my seed, and itself is
halted
And magnified thus, a still from the moving picture,
framed
In parting's hard embrace some beauty, flushed, fleshed,
tamed.
Separation's my metier, then, sifting through form the
formless:

DIALOGUE AT THE AIRPORT

Creation my end, to subdue and liberate time in the timeless.
I find the whole in elusive fragments: let one be caught
And profoundly known – that way, like a skeleton key, the
part
May unlock the intricate whole. What else is the work of
art?

II. Flight to Italy

The winged bull trundles to the wired perimeter.
Cumbrously turns. Shivers, brakes clamped,
Bellowing four times, each engine tested
With routine ritual. Advances to the runway.
Halts again as if gathering heart
Or warily snuffing for picador cross-winds.
Then, then, a roar open-throated
Affronts the arena. Then fast, faster
Drawn by the magnet of his *idée fixe*,
Head down, tail up, he's charging the horizon.

    And the grass of the airfield grows smooth as a fur.
The runway's elastic and we the projectile;
Installations control-tower mechanics parked aero-
                                planes –
Units all woven to a ribbon unreeling,
Concrete melts and condenses to an abstract
Blur, and our blood thickens to think of
Rending, burning, as suburban terraces
Make for us, wave after wave.

                          The moment
Of Truth is here. We can only trust,
Being as wholly committed to other hands
As a babe at birth, Europa to the bull god.
And as when one dies in his sleep, there's no divining
The instant of take-off, so we who were earth-bound
Are air-borne, it seems, in the same breath.
The neutered terraces subside beneath us.

FLIGHT TO ITALY

Bank and turn, bank and turn,
Air-treading bull, my silver Alitalia!
Bank and turn, while the earth below
Swings like a dial on the wing-tip's axis,
Whirls and checks like a wheel of chance!
Now keep your course! On azure currents
Let the wings lift and sidle drowsily –
A halcyon rocked by the ghost of the gale.
To watchers in Kent you appear as a quicksilver
Bead skimming down the tilted sky;
To the mild-eyed aircrew, an everyday office:
To us, immured in motion, you mean
A warm womb pendant between two worlds.

O trance prenatal and angelic transport!
Like embryos curled in this aluminium belly –
Food and oxygen gratis – again
We taste the pure freedom of the purely submissive,
The passive dominion of the wholly dependent.
Through heaven's transparent mysteries we travel
With a humdrum of engines, the mother's heartbeat:
And our foreshadowed selves begin to take shape, to be
Dimly adapted to their destination.
What migrant fancies this journeying generates! –
Almost we imagine a metempsychosis.

Over the Channel now, beneath the enchanting
Inane babble of a baby-blue sky,
We soar through cloudland, at the heights of nonsense.
From a distance they might be sifted-sugar-drifts,
Meringues, iced cakes, confections of whipped cream
Lavishly piled for some Olympian party –

A child's idea of heaven. Now radiant
All around the airscrew's boring penumbra
The clouds redouble, as nearer we climb,
Their toppling fantasy. We skirt the fringe of icebergs,
Dive under eiderdowns, disport with snowmen
On fields of melting snow dinted by the wind's feet,
Gleefully brush past atom-bomb cauliflowers,
Frozen fuffs of spray from naval gunfire.
    Wool-gathering we fly through a world of make-
                                    believe.
We *are* the aircraft, the humming-bird hawk moth
Hovering and sipping at each cloud corolla;
But also ourselves, to whom these white follies are
Valid as symbols for a tonic reverie
Or as symptoms of febrile flight from the real.
Let us keep, while we can, the holiday illusion,
The heart's altimeter dancing bliss-high,
Forgetting gravity, regardless of earth
Out of sight, out of mind, like a menacing letter
Left at home in a drawer – let the next-of-kin acknow-
                                    ledge it.

    The cloud-floor is fissured suddenly. Clairvoyance
It seems, not sight, when the solid air frays and parts
Unveiling, like some rendezvous remote in a crystal,
Bright, infinitesimal, a fragment of France.
We scan the naked earth as it were through a skylight:
Down there, what life-size encounters, what industrious
Movement and vocations manifold go forward!
But to us, irresponsible, above the battle,
Villages and countryside reveal no more life than

FLIGHT TO ITALY

A civilization asleep beneath a glacier,
Toy bricks abandoned on a plain of linoleum. . . .
　　After a hard winter, on the first warm day
The invalid venturing out into the rock-garden,
Pale as a shaft of December sunshine, pauses,
All at sea among the aubretia, the alyssum
And arabis – halts and moves on how warily,
As if to take soundings where the blossom foams and
　　　　　　　　　　　　　　　　　　tumbles:
But what he does sound is the depth of his own weak-
　　　　　　　　　　　　　　　　　　　　ness
At last, as never when pain-storms lashed him.
So we, convalescent from routine's long fever,
Plummeting our gaze down to river and plain,
Question if indeed that dazzling world beneath us
Be truth or delirium; and finding still so tentative
The answer, can gauge how nearly we were ghosts,
How far we must travel yet to flesh and blood.

　　But now the engines have quickened their beat
And the fuselage pulsates, panting like a fugitive.
Below us – oh, look at it! – earth has become
Sky, a thunderscape curdling to indigo,
Veined with valleys of green fork-lightning.
The atrocious Alps are upon us. Their ambush –
A primeval huddle, then a bristling and heaving of
Brutal boulder-shapes, an uprush of Calibans –
Unmasks its white-fanged malice to maul us.
The cabin grows colder. Keep height, my angel!
Where we are, all but terra firma is safe.
　　Recall how flyers from a raid returning,

Lightened of one death, were elected for another:
Their homing thoughts too far ahead, a mountain
Stepped from the mist and slapped them down.
We, though trivial the hazard, retract
Our trailing dreams until we have cleared these ranges.
Exalted, numinous, aloof no doubt
To the land-locked vision, for us they invoke
A mood more intimate, a momentary flutter and
Draught of danger – death's fan coquettishly
Tapping the cheek ere she turn to dance elsewhere.
Our mien is the bolder for this mild flirtation,
Our eyes the brighter, since every brush with her
Gives flesh a souvenir, a feel of resurrection.

Those peaks o'erpassed, we glissade at last to
A gentian pasture, the Genoan sea.
Look south, sky-goers! In flying colours
A map's unrolled there – the Italy
Your schooldays scanned once: the hills are sand-blond,
A pale green stands for the littoral plain:
The sea's bedizened with opening islands
Like iris eyes on a peacock's fan.
How slowly dawns on the drowsy newborn
Whose world's unworn yet – a firelit dress,
An ego's glamorous shell, a womb of rumours –
The first faint glimmering of otherness!
But half awake, we could take this country
For some vague drift from prenatal dreams:
Those hills and headlands, like sleep's projections
Or recollections, mere symbol seem.
          Then hurtling southward along shores of myrtle,

FLIGHT TO ITALY

Silverly circle the last lap,
My bull-headed moth! This land is nothing
But a mythical name on an outline map
For us, till we've scaled it to our will's dimensions,
Filled in each wayward, imperious route,
Shaded it in with delays and chagrins,
Traced our selves over it, foot by foot.
Now tighter we circle, as if the vertical
Air is a whirlpool drawing us down;
And the airfield, a candle-bright pinpoint, invites us
To dance ere alighting . . . Hurry! We burn
For Rome so near us, for the phoenix moment
When we have thrown off this traveller's trance,
And mother-naked and ageless-ancient
Wake in her warm nest of renaissance.

III. A Letter from Rome

We have been here three days, and Rome is really –
I know, I know; it would take three life-times to cover
The glorious junk-heap. Besides, our generation –
Well, you've only to think of James, as one must do
                                        here,
Lapping the cream of antiquity, purring over
Each vista that stroked his senses, and in brief
Rubbing himself against Rome like a great tabby,
To see what I mean. We who 'flowered' in the
                                        Thirties
Were an odd lot; sceptical yet susceptible,
Dour though enthusiastic, horizon-addicts
And future-fans, terribly apt to ask what
Our all-very-fine sensations were in aid of.
We did not, you will remember, come to coo.
Still, there is hope for us. Rome has absorbed
Other barbarians: yes, and there's nobody quite so
Sensuously rich and reckless as the reformed
Puritan . . . This by the way, to establish a viewpoint.
        You wanted my impressions. If only one were
A simple sieve, be the mesh close or wide,
For Rome to shake (and how it does shake one!),
                                        sifting
Some finer stuff from the coarser. But the trouble with
                                        me is
– Or perhaps it's the trouble with Rome – to dis-
                                        criminate

Merely between what is here and what has been here,
Between the eye and the mind's eye. The place has had
Over two thousand years of advance publicity
For us, which clouds the taste and saps the judgment.
What are you to do when Catullus buttonholes you
On the way to St. Peter's? When the Colosseum
presents

Nero[1] comparing notes with Roderick Hudson
On art and egotism? Sights, sounds, phantoms –
It is all too much for me, it should not be allowed!
    Perhaps, though, it is just here that something
emerges.

As when, composing a poem, the tangle of images
And jangle of words pressing hard on you, mobbing
you, may
Compel you to choose the right moment to disengage
And find the one word, the word of command which
makes them
Meekly fall in to their ranks, and the march continues:
So from this Rome, where the past lies weltering
In the blood of the present, and posters of Betty Grable
Affront the ghost of Cato; from all its grandiose
Culs-de-sac – the monumental gateways
That open on nothing, the staircases starting for
heaven,

The stone-blind palaces sweltering in the noon;
From the stilled tempest of the Sistine ceiling
To the water exasperated by sirocco
In every fountain basin; from the whole gamut,

---

[1] The Colosseum was built by Vespasian on the site of the Golden House of
Nero.

Theatrical, vulgar, rhetorical, fractious, sublime,
Of a city young as Tithonus, a city so ancient
That even the shadows here lie thick as dust: –
Emerges from all this, like invisible writing
Drawn out by the heart's warmth, one lucid word.

    Compost. I do not suppose the word original
(Original! Rome is quite beyond that). But think of it –
Century into century rotting down,
Faith piled on faith, Mithra on Jupiter,
Christ upon Mithra, Catholicism on Christ,
Temples imbedded in churches, church-stones in
                                     palaces:
Think of the pagan gods, demoted to demons,
Haunting and taunting the Early Fathers; long-dead
Lights of love, immortalized as Madonnas,
Demurely smiling at man's infant idealism.
Superstition, sanctity, cruelty, laws, art, lust –
Layer after layer laid down, course upon course
They renew the soul of this city, a city whose prospects
Are quarried out of its bones, a soul digesting
All foreignness into one rich dark fibre.
Rome, I can tell you, is the very type of
The hugger-mugger of human growth. For here
You can see the grand design eternally crossed
By the abject means, and its seedy ruin redeemed with
Valerian, arbutus, fennel; a character root-fast
Like a man's in the deposit of all his acts.

    Or say, a woman's; for so she appeared to us
On the first morning when we sauntered out
(The night before, wild strawberries and Frascati
Gold as the Roman May-light, cool as grottoes).

A woman – how shall I put it? – who makes you feel
She has waited two thousand years to meet you, and now
At once she is wholly yours, her liquid tongue,
Her body mantled in the full flush of Ceres,
And Primavera fluttering in her eyes.
She can be tiresome, no doubt, feverish, languid,
Changing her moods like dresses. But today
She has chosen to be divinely acquiescent:
'What shall we do?' the shell-like murmur comes,
'Shall we go shopping? Would you like me to show you
                              the sights?
'I will do anything you say, anything.'
. . . So we took, in the end, a carrozza to St. Peter's.
The driver was plainly a phantom; his conveyance
Jarred like old bones and mumbled of better days when
Violet-adorned beauties, sedate or giddy,
Turned all heads on the Corso. Thus we went
Jaunting over the seven hills of Rome
With the streets rocking beneath us as if seven ages
Turned in their grave, while noise upon noise the drift
Of our own – its voices, horns, wheels, bells, loud-
                              speakers –
Washed past us; then it dwindled away to a sea-shell
Cadence, beyond the Tiber, as we came near
Vatican city.
                    And now *vates tacete*
Should be the word. Words here can only scrabble
Like insects at the plinth of a colossus,
Scrabble and feebly gesticulate and go elsewhere.
Mere magnitude one might deal with, or pure and
                              simple

Meaning; but both in one, they give no purchase.
A dome superb as heaven's vault, capping a story
Whose hero blessed the meek; a desert of floor
Refracting faith like a mirage; the orchestration
Of gold and marble engulfing the still, small voice: –
You cannot pass over St. Peter's and what it stands for,
Whether you see it as God's vicarious throne
Or the biggest bubble ever yet unpricked.
And here, I have to confess, the old Puritan peeped out;
Not in sour protest against the Scarlet Woman,
Nor quite in the mood of my generation – its volatile
Mixture of hero-worship and disrespect;
But that an early habit of going to church
Prevents me from going to churches, however dis-
                                    tinguished
Their provenance, just as a sight-seer. Faith perhaps,
Though unconscious, is not yet dead, its breath still
                                    clouding
The glass of aesthetic perception. Apart from which,
I could not do with the guides who spring up like
                                    sweat-white
Fungi from every chink, and cling to one, furtively
Offering their curious knowledge; these pimps are not
The type you would choose to lead you to any altar.
So I was lost, ill at ease here, until by chance
In a side chapel we found a woman mourning
Her son: all the *lacrimae rerum* flowed
To her gesture of grief, all life's blood from his stone.
There is no gap or discord between the divine
And the human in that pieta of Michelangelo.

A LETTER FROM ROME

Then, after a marathon walk through the Vatican
galleries,
An endless belt of statues, tapestry, pictures
Glazing the eye, we came out into the streets again.
Better than all the museums, this strolling folk
Who sun themselves in the apricot light of antiquity
And take its prestige for granted. Cameo faces,
Contessa or contadina; bronze boys skylarking
As if they had just wriggled free from a sculptor's
hand —

How easily art and nature overlap here!
Another thing you would like about the Romans
Is the way they use their city, not as a warren
Of bolt-holes, nor a machine into which one is fed
Each morning and at evening duly disgorged,
But as an open-air stage. Palazzo, tenement
Seem pure façade — back-cloth for a continuous
Performance of business, love-making, politics, idling,
Conducted with a grand operatic extravagance
At the tempo of family theatricals. That same night
In the Piazza del' Esedra, sipping
Grappa, we watched the people, warm as animals
And voluble as fountains, eddying round
While the floodlit masonry was mere slabs of moon-
shine.
Rome is a city where flesh and blood can never
Be sacrificed, or mistaken, for abstractions.

But already (you can imagine how) my mind's
Crisscrossed with figures, memoranda, lightning
sketches,
Symbolic doodlings, hour by hour set down

Haphazardly as in Rome era on era.
And time is already shuffling tricks with discards.
Those fountains yesterday at the Villa d'Este
Grouped like patrician spectres in white conclave
Against a drop-scene of terraces and urns –
Did we indeed see them, or have they stepped
From a picture book years ago perused? Last night
We found on a wall of the Pincio a bas-relief,
A wide white calm imperious head suddenly
Surveying us out of the blank wall like some racial
Memory still not deep enough bricked up.

      Yesterday, then, was a day with the dead. We
                             hired
A car, and set out first for the Palatine hill.
The Forum? Well, picture a clearing found
In the depth of a clamorous forest, a low space littered
With bits of temples, arches, altars, mosaics
And God knows what – classical tags, fag ends,
Smatterings and stumps of a once apparently stable
Civilization, which packed up for all that
And left, like a gipsy encampment or picnic party:
And over it all, the silence of sheer exhaustion.
This area, sad as scar-tissue now, was the heart
Of a great republic, the S. P. Q. R.
Here they governed – a people, like the Scots,
Smouldering, pious, intolerant, living hard,
And demon fighters. Warlike was the seed;
But Time has pushed out this crop of decayed teeth.
It was the usual story. Long before
Their aqueducts ran dry and became picturesque,
Their virtue had imperceptibly seeped away

Into the dunes of ambition. They caught
Luxury, like a syphilis, from their conquests.
Then, feeling queer, they appointed one man to cure
them
And made a god of him. The disease was arrested
From time to time. But injections grew more frequent,
And the extremities began to rot;
While at home no amount of marble could hide the
sick core –
Vestals too free with their flame, tribunes long
impotent,
A rabble who had not the wherewithal to redeem its
Too often pledged heirlooms, justice and hardiness.
        So we were glad on the whole to leave this spot
Where glum mementoes of decline and fall
Are cherished like a grievance in Rome's heart,
And drive out towards Tivoli. The name
Had a certain frivolous charm for one oppressed
By dwelling on ruined greatness. The little town,
Modishly perched on an olive-tressed hillside,
Is famous for its sulphur springs (our driver
Stopped the car so that we might inhale it)
And of course, for the Villa d'Este. There at first
In the elaborate Renaissance gardens
Laid out for the lust of the eye, you seem to see
The lineaments of gratified desire.
An illusion though, like the smile on a dead face
Which means nothing but our own wish for peace.
Exquisite, yes: but a sense of the past, to be truly
Felicitous, demands some belief in the present,
Some moral belvedere we have not got.

This villa inhabited only by frescoes,
This garden groomed for sightseers – they mirror
Too clearly our lack of prospect or tenable premise.
The cardinals and princes who adorned them,
Lords of an age when men believed in man,
Are as remote from us as the Colosseum
Where high-tiered beasts howled down professional
heroes;
Perhaps – it is a comfortless thought – remoter.
      Back, then, to Rome. At Tivoli our driver
Stopped again like some house-proud, indelicate devil
To remark the smell of sulphur. Presently,
Held in a crook of Rome's old city wall
Close by St. Paul's gate under the pagan shadow
Of Gaius Cestius' pyramid, we found
The English cemetery. An ox-eyed, pregnant,
Slatternly girl opened the gate for us
And showed us round the desirable estate.
Here is one corner of a foreign field
That is for ever garden suburb. See,
In their detached and smug-lawned residences,
Behind a gauze of dusty shrubs, the English
Indulge their life-long taste for privacy.
Garish Campagna knocks at the back door,
Rome calls *en grande tenue*: but 'not at home'
Murmur these tombs, and 'far from home they died,
The eccentric couple you have come to visit –
One spitting blood, an outsider and a failure,
One sailing a boat, his mind on higher things.'
Somewhere close to the pyramid a loud-speaker
Blared jazz while we lingered at Keats' shabby mound,

But the air was drowned by the ghost of a nightingale;
The ground was swimming with anemone tears
Where Shelley lay.
                    We could feel at home here, with
This family of exiles. It is our people:
A people from whose reticent, stiff heart
Babble the springtime voices, always such voices
Bubbling out of their clay . . .
                         So much for Rome.
Tomorrow we shall take the bus to Florence.

IV. Bus to Florence

In the white piazza Today is barely awake
    A well-water breeze freshens
Her nakedness, musky with love, and wafts about
    Her breath of moist carnations.
Oh the beautiful creature, still in a dream pinioned,
    A flutter of meadowsweet thighs!
How she clings to the night, whose fingertips haunt her
                           waxen

    Body! Look at the eyes
Opening – pale, drenched, languid as aquamarines!
    They are open. The mere-smooth light
Starts glancing all over the city in jets and sparklets
    Like a charm of goldfinches in flight.
The tousled alleys stretch. Tall windows blink.
    Hour of alarum clocks and laces.
Sprinklers dust off the streets. The shops hum gently
    As they make up their morning faces.
And today comes out like a bride, a different woman,
    Subtler in hue, hazier,
Until the pensive mist goes, shyly avowing
    Such a zenith of shameless azure.

    This is our day: we mean
To make much of her, tune to her pitch. The enchant-
                       ing creature
    Travels with us. For once
There will be no twinge of parting in a departure.
    So eager she is to be off,

Spilling her armful of roses and mignonette,
    Her light feet restlessly echoed
From campanile and wristwatch (will they forget?
    Be late?) What a stir and lustre
Ripple the white square at a lift of her hand!
    Look! she has seen us, she points to
That blue bus with the scarab-like trailer behind.

We went the Cassian Way, a route for legions,
    We and the May morning.
Rome flaked off in stucco; blear-eyed villas
    Melancholiac under their awnings.
Rome peeled off like a cataract. Clear beyond us
    A vision good to believe in –
The Campagna with its longdrawn sighs of grass
    Heaving, heaving to heaven.
This young-old terrain of asphodel and tufo
    Opening its heart to the sun,
Was it sighing for death like Tithonus, or still athirst for
    Immortal dews? . . . We run
Towards Tuscany now through a no-man's-land where
                            stilted
    Aqueducts dryly scale
The distance and sport the lizard his antediluvian
    Head and tendril tail.
But soon the road rivers between flowerbanks:
    Such a fume and flamboyance of purple
Vetch, of campions, poppy, wild rose, gladioli,
    Bugloss! The flowery people,
Come out in their best to line our route, how they
                               wave

At the carnival progress! And higher,
The foothills flush with sainfoin, salutes of broom
    Are setting the rocks on fire.
Sutri, Viterbo, Montefiascone passed:
    Each village, it seemed, was making
A silent bar in the music, the road's hurdy-gurdy
    Winding, the tambourine shaking
Of sunlit leaves. You tatterdemalion townships –
    Elegance freaked with decay –
Your shuttered looks and your black doormouths
                                gaping

    Dumb in the heat of the day
Reject, unanswered, the engine's urgent beat.
    But now, groves of acacia
Swing their honeybells peal upon peal to welcome us
    Over the vibrant, azure,
Deep organ chords of Bolsena, the silvery wavelets
    Trilling tranquillamente.
That music followed us for miles, until
    We came to Acquapendente.

Eyes grown used to the light, we were finding our form
                          and meeting
    Impressions squarely.
Yet, where all was new, changeful, idyllic, it saddened
    To think how rarely
More than a few snippets remain from the offered fabric,
    And they not always
The ones we'd have chosen. It's sequence I lack, the
                          talent to grasp
    Not a here-and-there phrase

But the music entire, its original **stream** and logic. **I'd**
better

    Accept this, perhaps,
As nature's way: matter, the physicists tell one, is largely
    A matter of gaps.

Another stage, and a change of key. Listen!
    Rosetted oxen move –
The milky skins, the loose-kneed watersilk gait of
    Priestesses vowed to Love.
A road stubborn with stone pines. Shrines at the road-
side.

    A sandstone cliff, where caves
Open divining mouths: in this or that one
    A skeleton sibyl raves.
Signs and omens . . . We approached the haunts of
    The mystery-loving Etruscans.
Earth's face grew rapidly older, ravine-wrinkled,
    Shadowed with brooding dusk on
Temple and cheek. Mountains multiplied round us
    And the flowery guise shredded off as we
Climbed past boulders and gaunt grass high into
    A landscape haggard as prophecy,
Scarred with bone-white riverbeds like veins
    Of inspiration run dry.
Still what a journey away the apocalypse! See it –
    A tower, a town in the sky!
A child from the flowering vale, a youth from **the** foot-
hills

    May catch glimpses of death
Remote as a star, irrelevant, all of a lifetime

Ahead, less landmark than myth.
For ages it seems no nearer. But imperceptibly
      The road, twisting and doubling
As if to delay or avoid it, underlines
      That Presence: the man is troubled,
Feeling the road beneath him being hauled in now
      Like slack, the magnetic power
Of what it had always led to over the dreaming
      Hills and the fable of flowers.
So, while the bus toiled upwards and the Apennines
      Swirled like vapours about it,
That town in the sky stayed constant and loomed nearer
      Till we could no more doubt it;
And soon, though still afar off, it darkly foretold us
      We were destined to pass that way.
We passed by the thundercloud castle of Radicofani
      At the pinnacle of our day.

The wrack of cloud, the surly ruinous tower
Stubborn upon the verge of recognition –
      What haunts and weights them so?
      Memory, or premonition?
Why should a mouldering finger in the sky,
An hour of cloud that drifts and passes, mean
      More than the flowering vale,
      The volcanic ravine?
A driven heart, a raven-shadowing mind
Loom above all my pastorals, impend
      My traveller's joy with fears
      That travelling has no end.

But on without pause from that eyrie the bus, swooping,

48

Checking and swooping, descends:
The road cascades down the hillface in blonde ringlets
    Looped up with hairpin bends.
The sun rides out. The calcined earth grows mellow
    With place-names sleek as oil –
Montepulciano, Montalcino, Murlo,
    Castiglione. The soil
Acknowledges man again, his hand which husbands
    Each yielding inch and endures
To set the vine amid armies, the olive between
    Death's adamantine spurs.
Presently, on a constellation of three hills,
    We saw crowning the plain
A town from a missal, a huddle of towers and houses,
    Mediaeval Siena.
A gorge of a street, anfractuous, narrow. Our bus
    Crawled up it, stemming a torrent
Of faces – the faces impetuous, proud, intransigent
    Of those who had fought with Florence
For Tuscany. Was it a demonstration they flocked to?
    A miracle? Or some huger
Event? We left the bus stranded amongst them, a
                  monster
    Thrown up from their fathomless future,
And strolled into a far-off present, an age
    Where all is emblematic,
Pure, and without perspective. The twining passages,
    Diagrams of some classic
Doctrinal knot, lap over and under one another.
    The swan-necked Mangia tower
With its ruff stands, clear as Babel, for pride: beneath it,

Shaped like a scallop, that square
Might be humility's dewpond, or the rose-madder
    Shell from which Aphrodite
Once stepped ashore. And the west front of the
                               Duomo –
    How it images, flight upon flight, the
Ascending torrent, a multitude without number
    Intent on their timeless way
From the world of St. Catherine, Boccaccio and Fiam-
                               metta

    Towards the judgment day!

A township cast up high and dry from an age
    When the whole universe
    Of stars lived in man's parish
And the zodiac told his fortune, chapter and verse.
A simple time – salvation or damnation
    One black and white device,
    Eternity foreshortened,
Earth a mere trusting step from Paradise.
O life where mystery grew on every bush,
    Saints, tyrants, thrills and throes
    Were for one end! – the traveller
Dips into your dream and, sighing, goes.

After two hours we went on, for our destination
    Called. The adagio dance
Of olives, their immemorial routine and eccentric
    Variations of stance;
The vines that flourished like semaphore alphabets
                                endlessly

BUS TO FLORENCE

Flagging from hill to hill: –
We knew them by heart now (or never would), seeing
them tiny
And common as tormentil.
Florence invisibly haled us. The intervening
Grew misted with expectations,
Diminished yet weirdly prolonged, as all the go-between
World by a lover's impatience.
Through Poggibonsi we glided – a clown's name
And a history of hard knocks:
But nothing was real till at length we entered the
nonpareil
City . . . A hand unlocks
The traveller's trance. We alight. And the just coming
down to
Earth, the pure sense of arrival,
More than visions or masterpieces, fulfil
One need for which we travel.

This day, my bride of a day,
Went with me hand in hand the centuried road:
I through her charmed eyes gazing,
She hanging on my words, peace overflowed.
But now, a rose-gold Eve,
With the deep look of one who will unbosom
Her sweetest to death only,
She opens out, she flames and falls like blossom.
A spray that lightly trembles
After the warbler's flown. A cloud vibrating
In the wash of the hull-down sun.
My heart rocks on. Remembering, or awaiting?

v. Florence: Works of Art

Florence, father of Michelangelo,
Dante, da Vinci, Fra Angelico,
Cellini, Botticelli, Brunelleschi.
Giotto, Donatello, Masaccio! –

We shall not see their like, or yours, again.
Painters depart, and patrons. You remain,
Your bridges blown, your glory catalogued,
A norm for scholars and for gentlemen.

Reverend city, sober, unperplexed,
Turning your page to genius annexed
I breathe the mint and myrrh of Tuscan hills,
The tart aroma of some classic text.

Shields and medallions; overshadowing eaves
Like studious brows; the light that interleaves
Your past with amber: all's definitive, all
In changeless chiaroscuro one conceives.

I sometimes think the heart is ne'er so dead
As where some vanished era overspread
The soil with titan foliage, scattering down
Eternal rubies when its bloom was shed.

Where rode Lorenzo, panoplied and plumed,
Where Savonarola burned, and Ruskin fumed,
The lady artist sets her easel up,
The tourist with mild wonder is consumed.

FLORENCE: WORKS OF ART

Yet still the Arno navigably flows,
And saunterers past the Ponte Vecchio's
Jewel shops cast a shadow: here is still
A taste for life, a market for the rose.

Ah no, it's not the Florentines who fade
Before the statued loggia, the arcade,
The cliffs of floral stone. They live enough
In a pure tongue and a congenial trade.

Should the past overawe them? It's not theirs,
More than a mansion is the caretaker's.
A church by Giotto does as well as any
Other for this day's rendezvous or prayers.

What if along the pot-holed boulevards
Slogans are scrawled, not cantos? if postcards
Stand in for masterpieces, and ice cream
Says more to them than edifying façades?

The past is all-encroaching; and unless
They lopped its tentacles, stemmed its excess
To clear the air for some domestic seed,
They'd soon be strangled by a wilderness.

It's not the Florentine who pales beside
That vast, rank efflorescence. The pop-eyed
Tourist it is who rushes on his doom,
Armed with good taste, a Leica and a guide.

The primitive forest, the renaissance range
So massive are, surely they will estrange
Him from himself, or send him yelping home
To plastic novelties, to art's small change.

Plodding the galleries, we ask how can
That century of the Uncommon Man,
Sovereign here in paint, bronze, marble, suit
The new narcissism of the Also-Ran.

As many men, so many attitudes
Before the artifact. One writhes: one broods:
One preens the ego and one curls the lip:
One turns to stone, one to adjacent nudes.

Each man must seek his own. What do I seek?
Not the sole rights required by snob and freak,
The scholar's or the moralist's reward,
Not even a connoisseur's eye for technique;

But that on me some long-dead master may
Dart the live, intimate, unblinding ray
Which means one more spring of the selfhood tapped,
One tribute more to love wrung from my clay.

And if I miss that radiance where it flies,
Something is gained in the mere exercise
Of strenuous submission, the attempt
To lose and find oneself through others' eyes.

Singing Children: Luca Della Robbia

(T. H.)

I see you, angels with choirboy faces,
    Trilling it from the museum wall
As once, decani or cantoris,
    You sang in a carved oak stall,
Nor deemed any final bar to such time-honoured
                                    carollings
    E'er could befall.

I too gave tongue in my piping youth-days,
    Yea, took like a bird to crotchet and clef,
Antheming out with a will the Old Hundredth,
    Salem, or Bunnett in F.,
Unreckoning even as you if the Primal Sapience
    Be deaf, stone-deaf.

Many a matins cheerfully droned I
    To the harmonium's clacking wheeze,
Fidgeted much through prayer and sermon
    While errant bumblebees
Drummed on the ivied window, veering my thoughts to
    Alfresco glees.

But voices break — aye, and more than voices;
    The heart for hymn tune and haytime goes.
Dear Duomo choristers, chirping for ever
    In jaunty, angelic pose,
Would I had sung my last ere joy-throbs dwindled
    Or wan faith froze!

Judith and Holofernes: Donatello

(W. B. Y.)

... Next, a rich widow woman comes to mind
Who, when her folk were starving, dined and wined
Alone with Holofernes, until he
Grew rabid for her flesh. And presently,
Matching deceit with bitterer deceit,
She had struck off that tipsy captain's head
Upon the still untousled bed,
And borne it homeward in a bag of meat.

Old Donatello thought it out in bronze –
The wrists trailing, numb as it were from bonds;
The fuddled trunk lugged upright by a loop
Of hair; the falcon-falchion poised to stoop.
Tyrant, and tyrant's man, maybe:
Nevertheless, the sculptural face presents
A victim's irony, the mild innocence
Of passionate men whom passion has set free.

And she, the people's saviour, the patriot?
She towers, mouth brooding, eyes averted, not
In womanly compunction but her need
To chew and savour a vindictive deed;
Or so I construe it. One thing's sure –
Let a man get what issue he has earned,
Where death beds or love tussles are concerned
Woman's the single-minded connoisseur.

A political woman is an atrocious thing.
Come what may, she will have her fling
In flesh and blood. Her heady draughts cajole
A man only to cheat him, body or soul.
Judith took great Holofernes in.
For all the silver lamps that went before,
He made but a remnant on a knacker's floor:
She lives, the brazen kind of heroine.

Annunciation: Leonardo

(R. F.)

There was never a morning quite so tremendous again.
The birth, you think? I'm not for setting great store
By birth. Births aren't beginnings. And anyway
She only wanted to sleep off the pain
Which had made her a beast among beasts on the cow-
house floor.
Shepherds and magnates tiptoeing through the hay
(You get all kinds at an inn, she drowsily thought),
Even the babe – they were part of a snowdrift trance,
Almost unreal. He was to prove a good son
In his way, though his way was beyond her. Whatever
he sought
When he left home and led his friends such a dance,
He did not forget her as other boys might have done.

Her morning of mornings was when one flew to bring
Some news that changed her cottage into a queen's
Palace; the table she worked at shone like gold,

And in the orchard it is suddenly spring,
All bird and blossom and fresh-painted green.
What was it the grand visitor foretold
Which made earth heaven for a village Mary?
He was saying something about a Saviour Prince,
But she only heard him say, 'You will bear a child',
And that was why the spring came. Angels carry
Such tidings often enough, but never since
To one who in such blissful ignorance smiled.

Perseus Rescuing Andromeda: Piero di Cosimo

(W. H. A.)

It is all there. The victim broods,
Her friends take up the attitudes
  Right for disaster;
The winsome rescuer draws his sword,
While from the svelte, impassive fjord
Breaches terrific, dense and bored
  The usual monster.

When gilt-edged hopes are selling short,
Virtue's devalued, and the swart
  Avenger rises,
We know there'll always be those two
Strolling away without a clue,
Discussing earnestly the view
  Or fat-stock prices.

To either hand the crisis throws
Its human quirks and gestures.   Those
      Are not essential.
Look rather at the oafish Dread,
The Cloud-man come to strike it dead,
Armed with a sword and gorgon's head –
      Magic's credentials.

White on the rocks, Andromeda.
Mother had presumed too far.
      The deep lost patience.
The nightmare ground its teeth. The saviour
Went in. A winning hit. All over.
Parents and friends stood round to offer
      Congratulations.

But when the vast delusions break
Upon you from the central lake,
      You'll be less lucky.
I'd not advise you to believe
There's a slick op. to end your grief
Or any nick-of-time reprieve.
      For you, unlikely.

Boy with Dolphin: Verrocchio

(D. T.)

At the crack of spring on the tail of the cold,
  When foam whipped over the apple tree aisles
And the grape skin sea swelled and the weltering capes
             were bold,

59

I went to school with a glee of dolphins
Bowling their hoops round the brine tongued isles
And singing their scales were tipped by a sun always
revolving.

Oh truant I was and trident and first
Lord of fishes, bearleading all tritons
In the swim of my blood before the foam brewed bubble
burst.
And as I was nursling to mermaids, my sun
Cooed through their nestling grottoes a cadence
Of thrummed and choral reefs for the whale sounded gulfs
to hum.

Those were the gambolling days I led
Leviathan a dance in my sea urchin glee
Till the lurching waves shoaled out with a school of
wishes. My head
Was shells and ringing, my shoulders broke
Into a spray of wings. But the sea
Ran dry between two bars of foam, and the fine folk

In the temple of fins were flailed away
And the weed fell flat and the mermilk curdled,
And buoyant no more to bliss are the miles where alone I
play
My running games that the waves once aisled,
With a doll of a lithe dead dolphin saddled,
And cold as the back of spring is my tale of the applefroth
isles.

VI. Elegy Before Death: at Settignano

(To R. N. L.)

'. . . for be it never so derke
Me thinketh I see hir ever mo.'
CHAUCER

Come to the orangery. Sit down awhile.
The sun is setting: the veranda frames
An illuminated leaf of Italy.
Gold and green and blue, stroke upon stroke,
Seem to tell what nature and man could make of it
If only their marriage were made in heaven. But see,
Even as we hold the picture,
The colours are fading already, the lines collapsing
Fainting into the dream they will soon be.

Again? Again we are baffled who have sought
So long in a melting Now the formula
Of Always. There is no fast dye. Always? –
That is the word the sirens sing
On bone island. Oh stop your ears, and stop
All this vain peering through the haze,
The fortunate haze wherein we change and ripen,
And never mind for what. Let us even embrace
The shadows wheeling away our windfall days.

Again again again, the frogs are screeling
Down by the lilypond. Listen! I'll echo them –
Gain gain gain . . . Could we compel
One grain of one vanishing moment to deliver
Its golden ghost, loss would be gain

And Love step naked from illusion's shell.
Did we but dare to see it,
All things to us, you and I to each other,
Stand in this naked potency of farewell.

The villa was built for permanence. Man laid down
Like wine his heart, planted young trees, young
pictures,
Young thoughts to ripen for an heir.
Look how these avenues take the long view
Of things ephemeral! With what aplomb
The statues greet us at the grassy stair!
Time on the sundial was a snail's migration
Over a world of warmth, and each day passing
Left on the fertile heart another layer.

The continuity they took for granted
We wistfully glamourize. So life's devalued:
Worth not a rhyme
These statues, groves, books, bibelots, masterpieces,
If we have used them only to grout a shaken
Confidence or stop up the gaps of time.
We must ride the flood, or go under
With all our works, to emerge, when it recedes,
Derelicts sluggish from the dishonouring slime.

Our sun is setting. Terrestrial planes shift
And slide towards dissolution, the terraced gardens
Quaver like waves, and in the garden urn
Geraniums go ashen. Now are we tempted, each
To yearn that his struggling counterpoint, carried away

Drowned by the flood's finale, shall return
To silence. Why do we trouble
A master theme with cadenzas
That ring out, fade out over its fathomless unconcern?

Love, more than our holidays are numbered.
Not one day but a whole life is drained off
Through this pinprick of doubt into the dark.
Rhadamanthine moment! Shall we be judged
Self-traitors? Now is a chance to make our flux
Stand and deliver its holy spark, –
Now, when the tears rise and the levees crumble,
To tap the potency of farewell.
What ark is there but love? Let us embark.

A weeping firmament, a sac of waters,
A passive chaos – time without wind or tide,
Where on brief motiveless eddy seethe
Lost faces, furniture, animals, oblivion's litter –
Envelope me, just as the incipient poem
Is globed in nescience, and beneath
A heart purged of all but memory, grows.
No landfall yet? No rift in the film? . . . I send you
My dove into the future, to your death.

*   *   *

A dove went forth: flits back a ghost to me,
Image of her I imagine lost to me,
Up the road through Fiesole we first travelled on –
Was it a week or thirty years ago?
Time vanishes now like a mirage of water,
Touched by her feet returning whence she had gone,
Touched by the tones that darkly appeal to me,

The memories that make her shade as real to me
As all the millions breathing under the upright sun.

We are back at the first time we went abroad together.
Homing to this garden with a love-sure bent
Her phantom has come. Now hand in hand we stray
Through a long-ago morning mounting from a lather
Of azaleas and dizzy with the lemon blossom's scent.
And I seem to hear her murmur in the old romantic
                                                    way,
'So blissfully, rosily our twin hearts burn here,
'This vernal time, whenever we return here,
'To haunter and haunted will be but yesterday.'

I follow her wraith down the terraced gardens
Through a dawn of nightingales, a murmurous siesta,
By leaf-green frogs on lily leaves screeling again
Towards eve. Is it dark or light? Fireflies glister
Across my noon, and nightlong the cicadas
Whir like a mechanical arm scratching in the brain.
All yesterday's children who fleetingly caressed her
Break ranks, break time, once more to join and part us:
I alone, who possessed her, feel the drag of time's harsh
                                                    chain.

'Ah, you,' she whispers; 'are you still harping
'On mortal delusion? still the too much hoping
'Who needs only plant an acorn to dream a dryad's kiss?
'Still the doubtful one who, when she came to you
'Out of the rough rind, a naked flame for you,
'Fancied some knot or flaw in love, something amiss?'

Yes, such I am. But since I have found her
A revenant so fleshed in my memories, I wonder
Is she the real one and am I a wisp from the abyss.

Dare I follow her through the wood of obscurity –
This ilex grove where shades are lost in shade?
Not a gleam here, nothing differs, nothing sings,
                                    nothing grows,
For the trees are columns which ebonly support
A crypt of hollow silence, a subliminal thought,
A theorem proving the maggot equivalent to the rose.
Undiminished she moves here, shines, and will not fade.
Death, what had she to do with your futile purity,
The dogma of bone that on rare and common you
                                    would impose?

Her orbit clasped and enhanced in its diadem
All creatures. Once on a living night
When cypresses jetted like fountains of wine-warm air
Bubbling with fireflies, we going outside
In the palpitating dark to admire them,
One of the fireflies pinned itself to her hair;
And its throbbings, I thought, had a tenderer light
As if some glimmering of love inspired them,
As if her luminous heart was beating there.

Ah, could I make you see this subtle ghost of mine,
Delicate as a whorled shell that whispers to the tide,
Moving with a wavering watersilk grace,
Anemone-fingered, coral-tinted, under whose crystal-
                                    line

Calm such naiads, angel fish and monsters sleep or slide;
If you could see her as she flows to me apace
Through waves through walls through time's fine mesh
magically drawn,
You would say, this was surely the last daughter of the
foam-born,
One whom no age to come will ever replace.

Eve's last fainting rose cloud; mornings that restored her
With orange tree, lemon tree, lotus, bougainvillea:
The milk-white snake uncoiling and the flute's light-
fingered charm:
Breast of consolation, tongue of tried acquaintance:
A tranquil mien, but under it the nervous marauder
Slithering from covert, a catspaw from a calm:
Heaven's city adored in the palm of a pictured saint:
My vision's *ara coeli*, my lust's familiar,
All hours, moods, shapes, desires that yield, elude,
disarm –

All woman she was. Brutalizing, humanizing,
Pure flame, lewd earth was she, imperative as air
And weak as water, yes all women to me.
To the rest, one of many, though they felt how she was
rare
In sympathy and tasted in her warm words a sweetness
Of life that has ripened on the sunny side of the tree.
To herself a darker story, as she called her past to wit-
ness –
A heart much bruised, how often, how stormily sur-
mising
Some chasmal flaw divided it from whole felicity.

So I bless the villa on the hill above Fiesole,
For here and now was flawless, and the past could not
                                                    encroach
On its charmed circle to menace or to taunt her.
Oh, time that clung round her in unfading drapery,
Oh, land she wore like an enamelled brooch,
It was for remembrance you thus adorned her!
Now as I look back, how vividly, how gracefully
Ghosting there, she breathes me not the ghost of a
                                                    reproach.
Happiness, it seems, can be the best haunter.

You later ones, should you see that wraith divulged for
                                                    a moment
Through the sleep-haze of plumbago, glancing out
                                                    from the loggia's
Vain dream of permanence as from a page
Time is already turning again, will you thus com-
                                                    ment? –
'She is some dead beauty, no doubt, who queened here
                                                    awhile
'And clasped her bouquets, and shrinks to leave the
                                                    lighted stage:
'Not quite of the villa's classic period, though –
'Something more wistful, ironic, unstable in act and
                                                    style,
'A minor masterpiece of a silver age.'

But to me she stands out tall as the Torcello madonna
Against a mosaic of sunlight, for ever upholding
My small, redeeming love. But 'love is all',

She says; and the mortal scene of planets and tides,
Animals, grass and men is transformed, proved,
       steadied around me.
But her I begin to view through a thickening veil,
A gauze of tears, till the figure inscrutably fades –
As every vision must vanish, if we and it keep faith,
Into the racked, unappeasable flesh of the real.

    *   *   *

But look, the garden storm is stilled, the flood
Blinked away like a tear, earth reconciled to
Her molten birth-bed's long prophetic throes!
Her hills are lizards in their solid trance
Of sun and stone: upon each hill
Vine and olive hold the archaic pose:
Below, the bubble dome looks everlasting
As heaven's womb, and threading the eyes of bridges
Arno endlessly into the loom of oblivion flows.

A ghost, the mere thought of a shade, has done it.
Testing the shifty face of the Now with a dove, I found
Terra firma. Whatever in me was born to praise
Life's heart of blood or stone here reached its zenith,
Conjuring, staying, measuring all by that meek shade...
Now, love, you have tried on your phantom dress,
Return to nakedness!
Be breathing again beside me, real, imperfect!
Enmesh, enact my dream till it vanishes!

The oranges are going out? Tomorrow
Will light them up again. Tomorrow will call you
With nightingales; tomorrow will leave

ELEGY BEFORE DEATH

A rose by your plate, and freshen the plumbago's
Blue millinery and open a parasol
Of cedar for you, as it did for the first, ignorant Eve
Before exile or death was thought of. But we know well
On what tenure we have this garden. Each day's a
livelier
Paradise when each dawn is a reprieve.

I imagine you really gone for ever. Clocks stop.
Clouds bleed. Flames numb. My world shrunk to an
echoing
Memorial skull. (A child playing at hide-
And-seek suddenly feels the whole terrible truth of
Absence.)
Too keen the imagined grief, too dearly gained
Its proof of love. I would let all else slide,
Dissolve and perish into the old enigma,
If that could keep you here, if it could keep
Even your sad ghost at my side.

But gold and green and blue still glows before us
This leaf of Italy, the colours fixed
The characters formed by love. It is love's way
To shine most through the slow dusk of adieu.
Long may it glow within us, that timeless, halcyon halt
On our rough journey back to clay.
Oh, may my farewell word, may this your elegy
Written in life blood from a condemned heart
Be quick and haunting even beyond our day.

VII. The Homeward Prospect

TOM   A word with you, my friends. High summer is
scorching up
Northwards through poplared Umbria to these foothills of
Tuscany.
But I notice a nip in the air, a recession in all around me –
Statues and groves and fountains adopting a cooler attitude,
As if they were already waiving their claims upon us.

DICK   I feel – oh look at the stream's face, innocently
asleep
But twitching as if a nightmare coursed it! Stagnant as ice,
Bland as silver it seems now: but fast and faster the drift of
Objects inexorably drawn onward unmasks it. I feel
Time's force. It is a last reach. I know the tug of the weir.

HARRY   You should not take it to heart so, Dick. It is
merely one more
Holiday ending. Now is a chance to count the change,
To check the income against the outgoings, and find our
balance.
We shall come back some day – if only to demonstrate
Upon our person the law of diminishing returns.

TOM   Coming or going, I care not, when poised, alert and
shimmering
Like angels on a pinpoint, we stand at the tip of departure.

DICK   A point that is equidistant between two fields of
attraction
And thus, for me, the extreme agony.

HARRY   One or the other
Proves always the stronger field. You should regard such
                                                    occasions,
Dick, as limberings-up and rehearsals for a deathbed.

TOM   Well, God save us all! What a way to encourage
                                                the queasy
Traveller! We go home enriched

DICK   Sobered

HARRY   Lightened:
Lightened of one illusion, and therefore one truth the
                                                    richer.

TOM   Enriched with extravagant draughts of the strange:
                                        after them, soberer.

DICK   Sobered through sense of gain, by knowledge of
                                        loss enlightened –
Though what we have gained or lost is not yet apparent to
                                                        me,
Nor do I get any answer from these implausible word-plays.

HARRY   Time will tell. In the meantime, let us inquire
                                            what Tom,
The boyish and indiscriminate collector, has filled our trunk
                                                    with.

TOM   Sapphires of lakes I declare, a tiara of diamond fire-
                                                    flies,
Emerald valleys aglow in platinum dawns, mosaic of
Noondays, ivory evenings with voices flowing like thick silk:
Illuminated leaves torn from an Italian
Book of hours: frescoes and canvases by the masters;

A landscape with figures alive yet touched by the same genius:
Perfumes of contraband moments, essences of antiquity:
Nightingales, oxen, a hoopoe, cicadas and frogs – mis-
cellaneous
Curios rare as dirt and cheap as gold. I declare, too,
The wines of the country, the olive and maize of women's
flesh.

DICK   That will do to go on with. And such of these
acquisitions
As we get past the paternal customs and heavy duties
Which await our return, I shall unpack in the front parlour
Where Harry will arrange them in the pattern his latest
aesthetic
Or ethic requires, to show off to our guests, like any travel-
bore.
Presently, chipped and tarnished, or crowded out, they will
find
Their way to the attic: and there, one morbid afternoon
When rooks are eddying round a backwater of brackish sky
And a blight smears over the streets, morosely rummaging I
Shall cut myself to the bone on some poignant cobwebbed
souvenir.

HARRY   Let it be so. What Tom acquires for us has no
absolute
Value; nor, I admit, have the elegant systems wherein
I am disposed to compose it. There's no way even of telling
Which objects are really kin to us, which we've partaken of
life with,
Until, deep buried, they draw blood from us and are
eloquent.

Home is where we inter our travels, but equally give them
A chance to germinate beneath the dust and the housework,
The preoccupied face of routine, the protective sleep of the
                                                    heart.
Thence, on a gust of travail, something is born, crying
'I am your flesh and blood!' . . . Let us look homeward,
                                                    then.

TOM   I see, as the plane booms into the beetling, vertical
                                                    dark,
Gold and green and blue, amber and red, the lights of
A city like uncut gems in a jeweller's tray, tempting
And myriad below me. How precious now are the stones of
                                                    London!
How deeply caressing the velvet blackness in which they are
                                                    bedded!

DICK   Soon my bees will be swarming, swirling and
                                          swarming upward
Like bonfire sparks in a gale. Let the early flowers be
                                                    consumed,
The new cells built. I feel – and my harebell heart wind-
                                                    lessly
Quivers with far-flown tremors – the tramp, tramp of
                                                    Atlantic,
A funeral march plangent upon my uttermost shore.

HARRY   I imagine our house repainted by absence, the
                                          windowpanes cleaned,
A clearer view of the tangled streets, and the flowerbeds
                                                    tidier.
I return to myself as it were to a son who, in the interval,
Has grown perceptibly older, filled out; or like the astral

73

Self flying back to a body refreshed by the night's vacation.

TOM   Happy the natural nomad, sees home in a series of
new lights!

DICK   Blessed the born settler, whom all roads lead to
home!

HARRY   Can the human animal ever return, though, to
its old form?

TOM   Never. The form may remain; but the animal,
being a mere sequence
Of current sensations, could not recognize it.

DICK   You're wrong.
The *human* animal carries his form

HARRY   Like a shell?

TOM   Like a prison—
Where, but for me, you'd be starving in solitary confine-
ment.

DICK   Neither a shell nor a prison. Say rather an x, a
potential
Within him that cell by cell he has to incarnate, until
It sloughs him off one day and emerges, more or less perfect.

HARRY   That is not quite what I meant. I wonder, to be
explicit,
If the home to which our traveller returns may seem, not
only
Changed by his prodigal experience, but estranged from
him.

TOM   Why yes. And that is surely one of the points of
travelling:

The exotic veils we bring back and drape over the form of
The too familiar charmer, reviving her value, her mystery,
Compel us to woo her again.

DICK   I cannot take part in such make-believe.
Home, for me, is simply the place you can never quit;
An ideal home, if you like, which you spend a lifetime
building
Out of whatever comes to hand – dropped bricks, last straws,
Love's mortar, the timbre and rubble of today, old stones
from Italy.

HARRY I agree with you both, but will add *this*: our
going abroad is
Only a shift in space, a projection of home's shadow,
Unless it enlarges us with a new concept whereby
We may reassemble the known in a different, more lumin-
ous pattern,
The better to guide or follow our fateful thread of becoming.

TOM Must every holiday end in a kind of Royal Com-
mission?
I myself, like a sun-warmed stone or a satisfied lover,
Am purely grateful. Cannot one say so, and leave it at that?

DICK Grateful exactly for what? Italy waits a tribute.
HARRY Let us sharpen our recollections and write in
her visitors' book.

TOM On the sill of languorous autumn a tortoise-shell or
red admiral
Called by a sunbeam opens the eyes of its dreamless wings,
Longs for a last flutter, rustles against the windowpane
Trembling in the draught of a heliotrope desire.

Italy was the sun that awoke me, the hand that opened
A window and released me into a new playground.
I spread my wings on her basking stones, with her bells I
quivered,
Then sipped the violet mountains and the lilies of her
valleys:
On dome after dome alighting, pirouetting through grave
arcades,
Dithering over the fruit in a marketplace, pinned to a
frieze or
Skimming the dew of flesh, I wilfully everywhere wafted
Like a soul freed from a body yet fraught with the body's
enthralments.
I have no call to improve myself or the shining hour:
There was only the dance, the butterfly kiss on each of a
thousand
Adorable things. That dance is the tribute I pay to Italy.

DICK   On a flank of the hard-faced Apennines, on the
threshold of sheer desolation,
I see a few acres of terraced farmland, ruled with olives
And ridged between for cereal, not a foot nor a clod wasted,
All snug and rooted against the barbarian hordes of boulders.
It is a composite picture: many such have I seen here --
Places where generation on generation labouring
Up to the last instant before the rock takes over,
Ploughing their legends back into the heart's fibre,
Hammering their need to a tool and an emblem of primary
virtue,
Have kept man's nature green. It's here, and not in some
absolute

Immaculate distance or lawn of idyllic dance, I have found
The piety glimpsed by my youth, the deity under the fable.
And whenever, amid the vapours and topheavy crags of the
                                                    present,
I feel a handhold or lifeline, and grasp in myself the classical
Lineage of man's endurance, I shall remember Italy.

HARRY   On a lap of the road to Florence we passed a
                                    Tuscan graveyard
Out in the fields at the far end of a cortege of cypresses,
Insulated and distanced from life, yet part of a frieze where
Living and dead are one to love's creative eye,
Embryos each of the other . . . I took our most cherished
                                                    possession
And offered her to death. I took a ghost for my glass
And focused through it the inchoate, atomized face of
                                                    becoming.
Then, from the tower in the sky to the tiniest flower on the
                                                    earth's hem,
All was distinct, illustrious, full-formed in the light of
                                                    necessity,
Time's cocoon fallen away from the truth and kinship of all
                                                    things.
For one immeasurable moment the world's hands stood still
And the worm that ticks at the heart of the golden hoard was
                                                    silent.
Losing my heart to this alien land, I renewed my true love:
Lending my love to death, I gained this grain of vision.
I took my pen. What I wrote is thanks to her and to Italy.